BLACK MAMBAS

by Vicky Franchino

Children's Press®

An Imprint of Scholastic Inc.

Content Consultant
Dr. Stephen S. Ditchkoff
Professor of Wildlife Sciences
Auburn University
Auburn, Alabama

Photographs ©: cover: Maik Dobiey; 1: Jelger Herder, Buiten-beeld/
Minden Pictures; 1: Meriel Lland/Getty Images; 2 background:
Jens1948/Dreamstime; 2 inset: Meriel Lland/Getty Images; 3
background: Jens1948/Dreamstime; 3 inset: Meriel Lland/Getty Images;
4: Roger de la Harpe/Africa Imagery/African Pictures/The Image
Works; 5 background: Roger de la Harpe/Africa Imagery/African
Pictures/The Image Works; 5 top inset: Stuart G Porter/Shutterstock,
Inc.; 5 bottom inset: Balint Porneczi/Bloomberg/Getty Images; 6, 7:
blickwinkel/Alamy Images; 8, 9: Roger de la Harpe/Africa Imagery/
African Pictures/The Image Works; 10, 11: Meriel Lland/Getty
Images; 12, 13: reptiles4all/Shutterstock, Inc.; 14, 15: Stuart G Porter/
Shutterstock, Inc.; 16, 17: Peter Dawson/age fotostock; 18, 19: Karl H.
Switak/Science Source; 20: Jose Manuel Revuelta Luna/Alamy Images;
22, 23: Animals Animals/Superstock, Inc.; 24, 25: John Osborne/Alamy
Images; 26, 27: Adrian Warren/Ardea/Animals Animals; 28: Steven
Gilham/Alamy Images; 31: John Cancalosi/Alamy Images; 32, 33:
Skynavin/Shutterstock, Inc.; 34, 35: Heiko Kiera/Shutterstock, Inc.; 36:
Balint Porneczi/Bloomberg/Getty Images; 38, 39: Austin Stevens/age
fotostock; 40, 41: Heinrich van den Berg/Getty Images; 44 background,
45 background: Jens1948/Dreamstime; 45: Meriel Lland/Getty Images.

Library of Congress Cataloging-in-Publication Data
Franchino, Vicky, author.
  Black mambas / by Vicky Franchino.
    pages cm. — (Nature's children)
  Summary: "This book details the life and habits of black mambas"—
Provided by publisher.
  Includes bibliographical references and index.
  ISBN 978-0-531-21392-6 (library binding : alk. paper)
  – ISBN 978-0-531-21495-4 (pbk. : alk. paper)
  1. Black mamba—Juvenile literature. [1. Snakes.] I. Title. II. Series:
Nature's children (New York, N.Y.)
  QL666.O64F715 2015
  597.96'4—dc23   2014043960

Printed in China 62
SCHOLASTIC, CHILDREN'S PRESS, and associated logos are
trademarks and/or registered trademarks of Scholastic Inc.

1 2 3 4 5 6 7 8 9 10 R 25 24 23 22 21 20 19 18 17 16

Black Mambas

Class	Reptilia
Order	Squamata
Family	Elapidae
Genus	*Dendroaspis*
Species	*Dendroaspis polylepis*
World distribution	Southern and eastern Africa
Habitats	Found in grassy plains and wooded or rocky areas; sometimes nests in hollow trees or abandoned termite mounds
Distinctive physical characteristics	Grows to an average length of 6.6 to 8.2 feet (2 to 2.5 meters); has a coffin-shaped head; inside of mouth is black; skin is gray, brown, or olive
Habits	Active during the day; usually waits for prey instead of stalking; one of the world's fastest snakes
Diet	Carnivore; mostly eats small rodents and birds

BLACK MAMBAS

Contents

CHAPTER 1

A Dangerous Sight

A herd of Cape buffaloes gathers at the edge of a **savanna** to enjoy a lazy midday meal. The hot sun beats down, and all is quiet on the African plain. Suddenly, there are loud calls and sounds of distress. The buffalo begin to **stampede**! What's caused these animals to run? Did they catch sight of a hunting party or a group of lions? No. They spotted a black mamba, one of the world's most dangerous snakes.

The black mamba might not look that frightening at first glance. Its long, thin body is only about as wide as an adult human's thumb. But this snake's **venom** is extremely dangerous. Although this creature usually eats small **rodents** and birds, its venom can kill much larger animals. Just two drops can kill a person in less than 20 minutes. Animals of every size know to avoid the black mamba.

The black mamba is one of the world's deadliest animals.

Lengthy but Light

Like all snakes, the black mamba is a **reptile**. Reptiles are cold-blooded. This means they can't control their body temperature. On a cold day, a black mamba might lie in the sun to warm up. On a hot day, it hides in rock piles or slithers underground to stay cool.

Black mambas are found throughout southern and eastern Africa. They live in savannas, woodlands, and rocky areas. They like to live in protected spots. An abandoned **burrow** or termite nest or an area with fallen trees can all be good places for a mamba to make its **lair**.

At an average length of 6.6 to 8.2 feet (2 to 2.5 meters), the black mamba is the longest venomous snake in Africa. Despite this length, a black mamba weighs only about 3.5 pounds (1.6 kilograms) on average. This is because its body is thin.

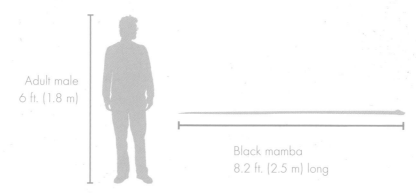

Adult male
6 ft. (1.8 m)

Black mamba
8.2 ft. (2.5 m) long

A black mamba hides among the grass in South Africa.

CHAPTER 2

Deadly Design

The black mamba has many features and abilities that help it survive and find prey. For example, large scales on the underside of the snake's body help it move along different surfaces, including soil, rocks, and tree bark. Black mambas usually travel on the ground, but they can also move easily in trees. A black mamba can slither at speeds of up to 12.5 miles (20 kilometers) per hour. This makes it one of the fastest snakes in the world.

The black mamba has two eyes that it uses to sense motion, but it can't see very well. Also, it doesn't have ears on the outside of its body. So how does it find prey? When an animal moves, it creates vibrations in the ground. A black mamba can feel these vibrations when it rests its head on the ground. The vibrations move through bones in the snake's lower jaw and into the mamba's special inner ear. The snake can then tell where nearby animals are and in which direction they are heading.

Black mambas often spend part of the day basking in a tree.

Moving Along

The black mamba's name does not come from its skin color. The skin on the top of the snake's body is usually a shade of gray, olive, or brown. The underside may be shades of white or yellow. It can be speckled or striped. So where does the black mamba get its name? The inside of its mouth is completely black!

Each year, as the black mamba grows it sheds its skin. If the snake has a good food supply, it will be able to grow faster. As a result, it will shed its skin more often. When a snake is getting ready to shed, its eyes will look cloudy and its scales will look dull. The black mamba rubs against a rough surface to remove its old layer of skin. The skin usually comes off in one big piece that looks like clear plastic. It's as if the black mamba were taking off a coat!

A black mamba flashes the black inside of its mouth when it feels scared or threatened.

An Unusual Way to Smell

As a black mamba slithers along, it quickly flicks its tongue in and out. This is how the snake detects odors in the air. A black mamba has a small nostril on each side of its head, but it uses them only to breathe. Tiny scent particles land on the snake's tongue when it darts out. When the mamba pulls its tongue back in, the tongue touches small holes on the roof of the snake's mouth. These holes lead to a structure called the Jacobson's organ. The Jacobson's organ sends a message to the part of the snake's brain that recognizes smells. This information tells the black mamba a lot about its surroundings. It could indicate that prey is nearby, that another mamba has recently passed through the area, or that danger is approaching.

FUN FACT! Snakes aren't the only animals with a Jacobson's organ. Many amphibians, mammals, and other reptiles have them, too!

Like other snakes, a black mamba's tongue is forked at the tip.

Fearsome Fangs

The black mamba's venom is extremely strong. It is a powerful mix of neurotoxins and cardiotoxins. Neurotoxins are substances that attack a victim's nervous system. This includes an animal's brain and spinal cord. Cardiotoxins are substances that damage the heart.

The black mamba relies on its fangs to inject venom into a victim's body. The fangs are sharp, hollow teeth at the front of the black mamba's mouth. The venom is produced in **glands** in the snake's head. It then travels through each hollow fang to its tip.

Some types of snakes have fangs that fold down when they close their mouths. A mamba's fangs do not move. As a result, they are quite short. If its fangs were longer, the black mamba would stab itself every time it closed its mouth.

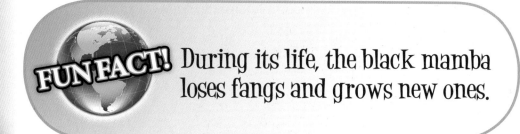

FUN FACT! During its life, the black mamba loses fangs and grows new ones.

A black mamba's fangs are much shorter than the fangs of other venomous snakes.

Time to Eat

Black mambas are **carnivores**. Their favorite prey includes small rodents such as voles, mice, squirrels, and rats. Black mambas sometimes also eat birds.

Black mambas hunt during the day and rest at night. They don't usually stalk their prey. Instead, they wait for their meals to come to them. When prey gets near, the black mamba springs out and bites it, injecting it with venom. If dinner is a mammal, the black mamba then simply waits for the animal to die. When the black mamba bites a bird, it holds on to it so the prey can't fly away.

Once the animal is dead, the black mamba swallows it whole in one big gulp. The snake can swallow prey whole because its jaws are connected by flexible tissue that can stretch very wide. The black mamba's saliva starts to break down the animal right away. The process is continued in the snake's stomach. It takes several days for the snake to completely digest its meal.

Black mambas do not chew their food. They swallow their prey whole.

On Guard

Most animals need to protect themselves and their young from **predators**. Because their poison is so deadly, black mambas have little to fear. They can easily kill animals that are many times larger than they are.

Humans are the black mamba's most dangerous predator. In Africa, there are many myths and folktales about the black mamba and how vicious and tricky it is. People are so terrified of black mambas that they often kill these snakes even if they do not pose a threat.

The black mamba's other major predator is the mongoose. Unlike other animals, the mongoose is **immune** to a mamba's venom. It often hunts black mamba eggs and newborns. Mongooses even attack adult mambas. Foxes, jackals, and large birds such as vultures can also be a threat to black mambas. Eggs and newborns are especially vulnerable to attacks.

The mongoose is well known for fighting venomous snakes.

Fair Warning

Black mambas are dangerous creatures. However, they would usually rather frighten an enemy than fight it. When threatened, a black mamba raises the front of its body off the ground to scare the other animal. Then it puffs out its neck to make itself look bigger and more threatening. Next, the black mamba opens its mouth wide and hisses. If the intruder still doesn't back off by this point, the black mamba will finally strike.

Humans who get bitten by black mambas need to get treatment right away. A person could die from a mamba bite in just 20 minutes, depending on how much venom entered his or her system. Black mamba bites must be treated using antivenom. Unfortunately, antivenom is very expensive, and it isn't always available where it is needed. Black mamba bites often happen in rural areas that are far from medical facilities.

Many animals, including the black mamba, make themselves look bigger to scare off attackers.

CHAPTER 3

Alone but Not Lonely

Black mambas usually spend their entire life within a small area called a **home range**. The size of a snake's home range depends on how much food and shelter is available. In areas where there is more food, a mamba does not need to travel far in search of a meal. In areas where food is less common, a mamba might need to expand its home range so it can get enough to eat.

When it is not moving around its home range, a black mamba stays hidden in a sheltered area called a lair. A lair might be underground or inside a hollow log. A mamba often returns to the same lair each day.

Black mambas are not social creatures. They usually do not spend time around other mambas. The only time they seek one another's company is when it is time to **mate**.

A good lair is one in which a snake is safe and well hidden.

The Mating Game

Black mambas mate in early spring. When a female mamba is ready to mate, she leaves a scent trail along the ground. A male black mamba finds her by following this trail. He flicks his tongue in and out of his mouth to track the smell. When he finds the female, he flicks his tongue over her body to make sure she is ready to reproduce.

Sometimes more than one male discovers a female's trail. If that happens, the males might fight to decide which one will mate with the female. During this fight, the male snakes raise the front part of their bodies off the ground. They then wrap their bodies around each other in a sort of fighting dance. The winner is the snake that can pin the other one to the ground.

After mating, the male and female do not continue socializing. They return to their solitary lifestyles.

Two male black mambas fight over a mate in Rwanda.

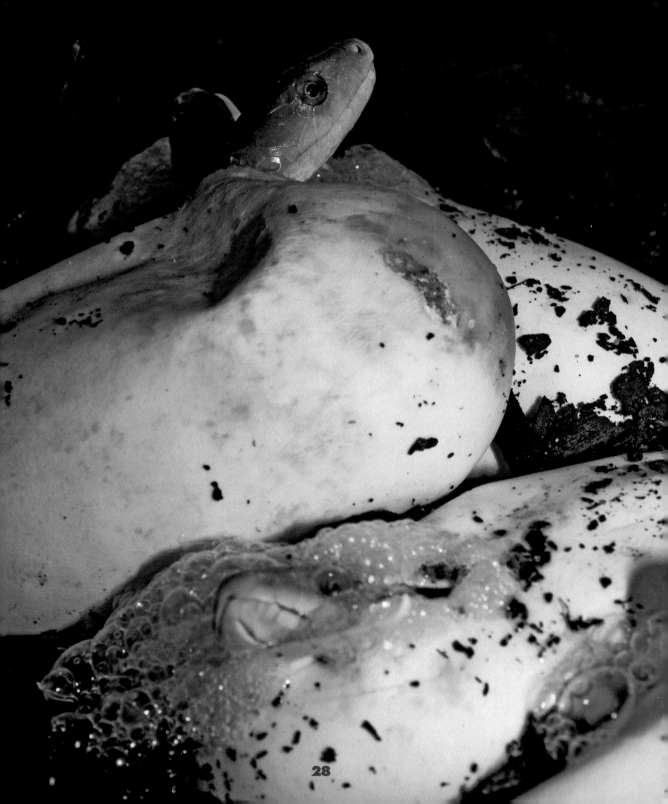

Here Come the Babies

Black mambas are oviparous. This means they lay eggs outside their body. About two to three months after mating, a female black mamba is ready to lay her eggs. She must find a safe place for the eggs to develop. She will not protect her eggs, so it is important to hide them from predators.

The perfect spot is warm and humid. A female mamba often lays her eggs in rotting plants. As the plants **decompose**, they give off heat and moisture that help the eggs develop.

It takes two to three months for the baby black mambas to grow inside their eggs. When it's time to hatch, a baby mamba uses a special egg tooth to tap its way out of the shell. Its mother is not around to protect and feed it. However, baby mambas have poisonous venom at birth. This means they can feed and protect themselves immediately.

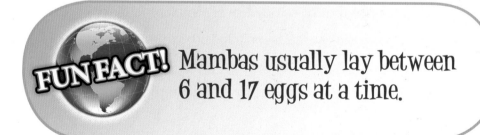

FUN FACT! Mambas usually lay between 6 and 17 eggs at a time.

Baby black mambas hatch from their soft-shell eggs.

CHAPTER 4

The Family Tree

Fossils show that the first snakes appeared on Earth more than 90 million years ago. Some of these ancient **species** shared the planet with dinosaurs.

Snakes' bodies have **evolved** over time. For example, snakes' earliest **ancestors** had legs. Over time, they changed to look like today's snakes. Now black mambas move by pushing their bodies sideways over the ground.

Black mambas' eggs have probably changed, too. Ancient reptiles had eggs without shells that could survive in the water. Having eggs with a shell allowed the black mamba to live on land, because the hard shell was protective.

Another feature that developed over time is the black mamba's venom. Other animals have legs to run away from an attacker or claws to protect themselves with. A black mamba is safe from almost every animal because its venom is so strong.

This 50-million-year-old snake fossil was found in Wyoming.

Explaining Elapids

The black mamba is a member of the Elapidae family. This snake family has more than 300 members. Other elapids include taipans, coral snakes, and cobras. All members of the family have some things in common. They have short fangs that don't fold up. They have powerful venom. Most only attack humans when they feel threatened. Some live on land, and others live in the water. Most lay eggs, but some give birth to live babies.

The king cobra is one of the best-known elapids. Reaching lengths of up to 18 feet (5.5 m), it is the longest venomous snake on Earth. Like the black mamba, it rises off the ground and puffs out its neck when threatened. Unlike the mamba, this snake does not desert its eggs after laying them. Instead, it builds a nest and protects its babies until they hatch.

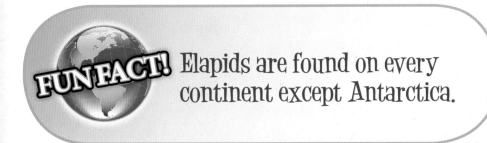

FUN FACT! Elapids are found on every continent except Antarctica.

A king cobra is easy to identify by the large hood at its head.

More Mambas

The black mamba is not the only type of mamba. There are also three green mamba species. Like the black mamba, they are extremely venomous and have a coffin-shaped head. Unlike the black mamba, they prefer to live in trees and aren't known to attack humans. And yes, they are all green!

The East African green mamba lives in the eastern and southern parts of Africa. It is the smallest mamba. It usually grows to between 4 and 6 feet (1.2 and 1.8 m) long. This mamba eats birds, eggs, small mammals, and sometimes lizards.

The West African green mamba lives in western Africa, from Senegal to Nigeria. It makes its home in coastal areas and forests. This mamba is usually about 6 to 7 feet (1.8 to 2.1 m) long. Its diet includes birds and lizards. Sometimes it falls onto its prey from a tree!

The Jameson's mamba lives in central Africa. It likes to eat lizards, frogs, birds, eggs, and small mammals. This mamba is usually no more than 6 feet (1.8 m) long.

A green mamba watches from its perch in a tree.

CHAPTER 5

Humans and Mambas

When people think about black mambas, they usually think about how dangerous or scary the snakes are. They might not know what an important role snakes play in controlling pests. Rodents are the black mamba's favorite food. These animals eat crops and spread disease. Without the black mamba, rodent populations could explode. This would be very dangerous in many of the poor areas where the black mamba lives. Ruined crops would cause major food shortages. Also, there is a lack of medical treatment in some of these areas. Diseases spread by rodents would likely harm huge numbers of people.

It is almost impossible to know how many black mambas there are. Scientists don't believe there is any reason to worry they will become **extinct** in the near future. However, this could change as humans clear wild land to make room for buildings, roads, and farms.

Researchers have studied black mambas both in labs and in the wild.

A Future in Medicine

Antivenom is a special medicine used to treat poisoning from snakebites. The most important ingredient in antivenom might be surprising. It is snake venom! To gather the venom, a handler "milks" a snake. The handler carefully holds the black mamba's head and presses its fangs against a glass. The venom leaks out.

Venom might also have other medicinal uses. Snake venom contains substances that block messages from the body to the brain. This helps control pain. Scientists believe that these substances could be used to create medications for people who are in a lot of pain. Scientists want to make new medicines to treat pain because the current ones often have side effects. Scientists have already tested medications made with black mamba venom. They are excited about the results. Doctors might one day use the venom of this feared creature to help people who are in pain!

Milking a snake—particularly a black mamba—is a dangerous process.

Spreading the Word

Many people are working to educate others about ways to deal with mambas safely and respectfully. Thea Litschka-Koen lives in Swaziland, a country in Africa that is home to many black mambas.

Litschka-Koen goes to homes and farms and catches black mambas. She teaches people to escape instead of killing the snakes. She also teaches people to get to hospitals as soon as possible if they are bitten. Litschka-Koen wants to make it easier for people who are bitten by black mambas to quickly get lifesaving antivenom. She has set up a charity called Antivenom Swazi. It raises money to create antivenom banks for people who cannot afford treatment.

Through the work of Litschka-Koen and others like her, more people will learn to live peacefully alongside black mambas. These incredible animals will be free to continue slithering through their African habitats for many years to come.

A black mamba glides out of a plant pot lying in a national park in Namibia.

Words to Know

ancestors (AN-ses-turz) — ancient animal species that are related to modern species

burrow (BUR-oh) — a tunnel or hole in the ground made or used as a home by an animal

carnivores (KAHR-nuh-vorz) — animals that eat meat

decompose (dee-kuhm-POZE) — to rot or decay

evolved (i-VAHLVD) — changed slowly and naturally over time

extinct (ik-STINGKT) — no longer found alive

family (FAM-uh-lee) — a group of living things that are related to each other

fossils (FOSS-uhlz) — the hardened remains of prehistoric plants and animals

glands (GLANDZ) — organs in the body that produce or release natural chemicals

home range (HOME RAYNJ) — the area to which an animal usually confines its daily activities

immune (i-MYOON) — if you are immune to a disease, you don't get sick from it

lair (LAIR) — a wild animal's resting place or den

mate (MAYT) — to join together to produce babies

predators (PREH-duh-turz) — animals that live by hunting other animals for food

prey (PRAY) — an animal that's hunted by another animal for food

reptile (REP-tile) — a cold-blooded animal that crawls across the ground or creeps on short legs; most have backbones and reproduce by laying eggs

rodents (ROH-duhnts) — animals with large, sharp front teeth that are constantly growing and used for gnawing

savanna (suh-VAN-uh) — a flat, grassy plain with few or no trees

species (SPEE-sheez) — one of the groups into which animals and plants of the same genus are divided; members of the same species can mate and have offspring

stampede (stam-PEED) — to make a sudden, wild rush in one direction, usually out of fear

venom (VEN-uhm) — poison produced by some snakes and spiders; venom is usually passed into a victim's body through a bite or sting

Habitat Map

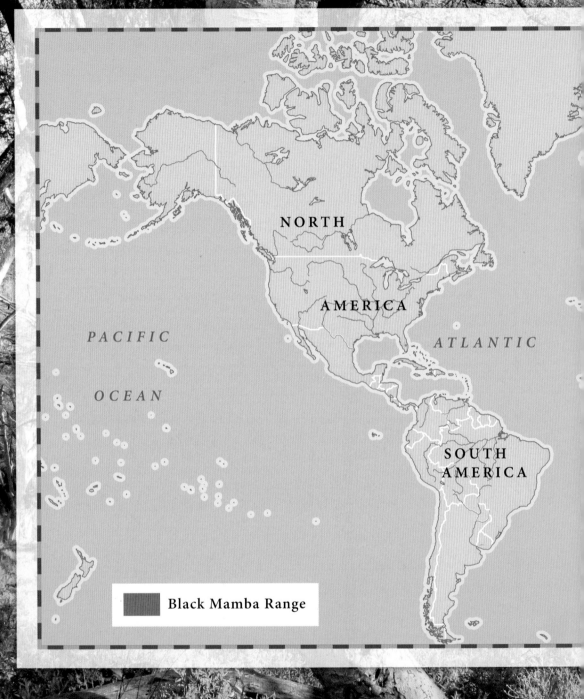

NORTH AMERICA

PACIFIC OCEAN

ATLANTIC

SOUTH AMERICA

Black Mamba Range

ARCTIC OCEAN

EUROPE

ASIA

AFRICA

PACIFIC OCEAN

INDIAN

OCEAN

OCEAN

AUSTRALIA

Find Out More

Books

Owings, Lisa. *The Black Mamba*. Minneapolis: Bellwether Media, 2013.

White, Nancy. *Black Mambas*. New York: Bearport, 2009.

Visit this Scholastic Web site for more information on black mambas:
www.factsfornow.scholastic.com
Enter the keywords **Black Mambas**

Index

Page numbers in *italics* indicate a photograph or map.

(Index continued)

About the Author

Vicky Franchino has never been to Africa and has never seen a black mamba (and that is okay with her!). She is sure that she would be quite terrified if she saw one up close—though she would try to remember to back up slowly and not panic! Vicky doesn't mind snakes in general as long as they are very small and not inside her house. Vicky lives in Madison, Wisconsin, with her family.

Photo by Kat Franchino